Ascending Order

Akron Series in Poetry

Also by William Greenway

Pressure Under Grace
Where We've Been
Father Dreams
Rain in Most Places
How the Dead Bury the Dead
Simmer Dim

Akron Series in Poetry

Elton Glaser, Editor

Barry Seiler, *The Waters of Forgetting*
Raeburn Miller, *The Comma After Love: Selected Poems of Raeburn Miller*
William Greenway, *How the Dead Bury the Dead*
Jon Davis, *Scrimmage of Appetite*
Anita Feng, *Internal Strategies*
Susan Yuzna, *Her Slender Dress*
Raeburn Miller, *The Collected Poems of Raeburn Miller*
Clare Rossini, *Winter Morning with Crow*
Barry Seiler, *Black Leaf*
William Greenway, *Simmer Dim*
Jeanne E. Clark, *Ohio Blue Tips*
Beckian Fritz Goldberg, *Never Be the Horse*
Marlys West, *Notes for a Late-Blooming Martyr*
Dennis Hinrichsen, *Detail from* The Garden of Earthly Delights
Susan Yuzna, *Pale Bird, Spouting Fire*
John Minczeski, *Circle Routes*
Barry Seiler, *Frozen Falls*
Elton Glaser and William Greenway, editors, *I Have My Own Song for It: Modern Poems of Ohio*
Melody Lacina, *Private Hunger*
George Bilgere, *The Good Kiss*
William Greenway, *Ascending Order*
Roger Mitchell, *Delicate Bait*
Lynn Powell, *The Zones of Paradise*

Ascending Order

William Greenway

The University of Akron Press
Akron, Ohio

All inquiries and permissions requests should be addressed to the publisher,
The University of Akron Press, Akron, OH 44325–1703

LIBRARY OF CONGRESS CATALOGING-IN-PUBLICATION DATA

Greenway, William, 1947-
    Ascending order / William Greenway.— 1st ed.
      p.   cm. — (Akron series in poetry)
    ISBN 1-931968-03-9 (pbk. : alk. paper)
    I. Title.   II. Series.
  PS3557.R3969 A93 2003
  811'.54--DC21

                    2003005696

Manufactured in the United States of America.
The paper used in this publication meets the minimum requirements of American National
Standard for Information Sciences—Permanence of Paper for Printed Library Materials,
ANSI Z39.48–1984. ∞

Cover design by Jodi Arment.
Cover illustration: *The Tower of Babel*, Peter Bruegel de Oude (the Elder). Courtesy of
Museum Boijmans Van Beuningen, Rotterdam.

For Betty

Acknowledgments: *And What Rough Beast: Poems at the End of the Century*, Ashland Poetry Press (1999): "Mississippi Moon"; *Anthology of Magazine Verse and Yearbook of American Poetry*, Monitor Book Company (1997): "Sugar"; *Artful Dodge*: "Lust at Christmas"; *Artword Quarterly*: "Before the Fire"; *Blue Mesa*: "The Dead Go on Before Us," *"The Leg of Mutton Nude,"* "Ennui"; *Cumberland Poetry Review*: "Tests"; *DAYbreak*: "Ascending Order"; *Ekphrasis*: "In the National Gallery," "White Buildings by Water with Steps Going Down"; *HQ Poetry Magazine: The Haiku Quarterly*: "My Father, Driving South"; *Incliner*: "First Impression"; *The Laurel Review*: "Still Life with Chili and Onions," "Lamb of God, Inc."; *Louisiana Literature*: "My Father, Driving South"; *Maryland Poetry Review*: "Mississippi Moon"; *Mid-American Review*: "The End of Loving," "The Punishment of Days"; *New Welsh Review*: "The Last Annual Dead Celebrity Charity Golf Tournament"; *Planet*: "Cupidity," "If Thou Hadst Been Here, My Brother Had Not Died," "Lamb of God, Inc.," "Priscilla"; *Poetry*: "Aesop at Sixty," "Running the Body," "Them"; *Poetry Northwest*: "A Woman Brought to Child," "The Poet, Calling the Kettle Black"; *Prairie Schooner*: "Deadbeats"; *Rhino*: "Author of the Year," "I Have Chosen You out of the World"; *Slant*: "The Second Verse"; *Southern Review*: "Prostrate"; *Spoon River Poetry Review*: "Hell's Garage," "Sugar"; *Texas Review*: "My Pills"; *2001: A Science Fiction Poetry Anthology*, Anamnesis Press (2001): "Them."

I thank Youngstown State University for the Faculty Improvement Leave and the Research Professorship that allowed me to write this book.

Contents

I

The Dead Go on Before Us

My Father, Driving South

He'd pull us by the toes in the dark,
3 A.M., but we rose gladly as if we would be
transfigured by distance, by the car trunk
solid with beach chairs and suitcases.
We knew we'd wake in Valdosta, moss
on the trees, coffee steaming evaporated milk,
then sleep again, pillows fattening beneath
our dreaming heads like marshmallows.

When we woke again, it would be Lake City,
the land flat in sun, the roads sea-shelled and blinding,
palm trees, and we'd be almost to the sea,
a place almost as good as the going—
when my father's silhouette in the front seat
already wore his captain's hat, my mother
was happy for once, and I fell asleep
to the surf of passing cars that played slow lightning
over the ceiling, the moon almost full
like a candled egg.

Lamb of God, Inc.

The churches my father built
are still there, out on the crosses
of country roads. He wanted
to be a preacher, but, unschooled,
no congregation would have him
for long, so he made churches to
call God down, to hold him inside.
The other wood butchers
would go to a juke joint
and get drunk after work
while I went to college: *You're
one of them educated fuckers, ain't ya?*
Once I climbed up inside the spire
to nail, and the ladder cracked.
I jumped free, fell two stories,
and landed on my feet.

The jobs never came in under cost,
so eventually he lost it all,
including our house.
Then his heart quit.
He always bought everyone
a ham at Christmas.
Every summer, I would climb
the half-fleshed bones of another
church with a pack of black
shingles on my shoulder
like sixty pounds of sins
while God floated out
through the open roof.

I Have Chosen You out of the World

His whole life my preacher
father fought the mechanical:
the mimeo troll drooling blue
in the basement of our church, wadding
the weekly bulletin; his typewriter
clattering like a combine bringing
in the sheaves, leaving the smudge
of ribbon ink on onionskin—the material
world laying for him everywhere.
When the top stuck down on
the borrowed convertible he drove
for the Bible School parade,
me and Momma watched him sit
in the rain at every stoplight
and punch the wet leather seats.

He was waiting for a better
world, the pulleys pure
thought, the rotors running smooth
as Ezekiel's wheel, the souls of machines
gliding, like my computer,
on electrons, all our regrets
living somewhere in air
until they're ready to alight
and align themselves darkly
on the page, like crows
in the snowy fields.

Deadbeats

The calls came after dinner, and for years
he tried to muffle their breath with
the breadth of his body, though the seep
of angry voices filled our kitchen
like the drip of dirty water—all the things
he floated on a life he couldn't afford, my mother's
Corvette, new houses in the suburbs.
He even owed *me* two hundred.

I got to call them back
when he died, hear their sighs, resigned,
the perfect epitaph: *Let the Bastards Collect*
Now, the knot of his life coming
clear with the twitch of one string.

And now my sister, too, has died
in my debt. Creditor, I write off
what they owed—dues, attention,
apologies, though I would send dun
hounds of hell or heaven to harry
them, haul them back
to what they've left unpaid,
or relieve me of this bag I'm left
holding, heavy with all
I owe them and can never repay.

Lot

To help me through college,
my father let me work
in his bookstore, the last

of many failures
of a failed preacher.
The strange books sat on shelves

of pressed board: real wood
splintered and glued
back together. We shared

the building with a man
who sold fish dip, and the Welcome
Wagon woman. Occasionally,

customers would come in
but seldom bought, probably
because I pretended I didn't see them

and kept writing poems, embarrassed by
After the Rapture, Angels
Are Real, Jesus Is a Millionaire.

I became a professor,
and my father died
of a heart attack

after he'd had to go back
to being an accountant.
He's buried not far

from that southern strip mall
where the parking lot sizzled
in the summer sun like Sodom.

A Woman Brought to Child

The second law is that the bad news is always
worse than the good news is good:
I won a prize,
and my only sister, Sherry, died.

She never had a chance.
I remember cowering while
our parents upstairs screamed
at each other again about her grades, until
she stood up, threw down her schoolbooks,
and began screaming, too.
If anything happened, it happened
to her: nickname Stinky, coonskin cap
with the plastic pate stamped Davvy
Crockett, tonsils, appendix, wren
bones breaking, green eyes behind
bat-wing glasses, the boys
staying away. Algebra
chased her from nursing school
like nausea, then a brick Bible
college, a redneck marriage, and losing
her babies to the county.

Barmaid, she was trying
to start again when I left her
drunk on the doorstep that
Christmas ten years ago, gave me that old
picture of herself as Shirley Temple
with a cowboy hat, white taps, red

sequined cuffs that swayed to "Pony Girl."
Her new man stayed inside with his
cartoons and vodka in that month's
dump, as she said goodbye
for the last time, hugged her new
daughter, wept, and waved.

You know the story—it's the one
the private eye tells about finding
the guilty, who done in the floating
body of the woman with no last name,
the first something rich, like Candy
or Ginger, who somehow got lost
and fell in with bad companions.
Somewhere near the end of the movie,
the gumshoe finally tracks the fictional family
down and shows them the picture
of the woman they hardly recognize, yellow
and withered, and they show him the picture
of the little girl they remember—
squinting into the sun, standing
in the doorway to the rest of her life, waving
goodbye, her jelly bread falling
jelly side down.

If Thou Hadst Been Here,
My Brother Had Not Died

*For whoever shall do the will of my Father who is in
heaven, he is my brother, and sister, and mother.*

—Matthew 12:50

My family believed that family
didn't matter, that only the damned, like
our neighbors and the Mafia,
had faith merely in each other. Hadn't Jesus,
when his mother asked to see him,
looked around at the new Christians
squatting at his feet and said, *These
are my family of the spirit*?
So the Lord would be proud of us now,
scattered, dead, disconnected, each of us
having waited in our separate fields
for a lonely rapture of love or liquor
or poems. The old movie last night starred
Raymond Burr before he weighed
three hundred pounds, and Robert Mitchum
before that squashed look around the mouth
that shows he either has false teeth
or needs them, the way Daddy looked
near the end because he never
took care of himself. Nor have we.
Who knows what family lost or saved
has to do with any of this, except

that the only thing we ever did together
was watch old movies. So when my sister died,
and her daughter had no other number to call,
I thought of Fay Wray, Bruce Cabot, even Robert Armstrong,
all of them tracked down and destroyed more thoroughly
than any mere monster could, and I finally knew
why Kong, climbing to meet his death,
reached through the skyscraper window, feeling
for Fay, a woman he could never fuck,
to take her with him as high as he could go, high
as Jesus on the mountaintop, ascending alone.

The Second Verse

When my father died, I did okay, even
joked around the casket, just another
family reunion, and then the long ride
to the church. It was the second verse
of his favorite hymn when I came apart
like a cheap watch, held my head
and trembled: *When we've been there
ten thousand years, bright shining as the sun.*

Even when I was little, I'd ask how long
eternity was: "Forever and ever," he'd answer.
"But how long?" And then, "What do you do?"
"Praise the Father," he'd say, and I'd think,
but I already have a father.

And, oh, how we'd argue when I
was grown, he quoting scripture, and I,
smartass, newly pagan grad student,
countering with *Earth's the right place
for love: I don't know where it's likely
to go better.* Our last fight was over
Super Bowl III, Broadway Joe with his long
hair, fur coat, women, and white shoes,
and crew-cut Earl Morral who wore black
high-tops like Li'l Abner and drank only milk.

Today, driving along, it came on
the radio, and, surely cured

at last, I didn't change stations,
but began to sing along. And then
the second verse, and the road
blurred, and the sun became that
misty glow all those nut cases say
they walk toward in death, but then
come back from, all those
Lazaruses who, with eternity
in sight, hold their heads
and tremble, run back down
the path of light to the world
of time, of sorrow and suffering,
and hymns, and milk, and fathers.

The Child Suicides

They tied somebody's daddy's good white
handkerchief over my eyes like a hostage, spun me,
and I Frankensteined after those voices
whirling around and away. In my dark,
I began to dream the tinkle
of an ice cream truck: *Oh the moon shines*
tonight on pretty Redwing, and then
I fell like Alice and came to
at the foot of the tall wall by our
driveway, the handkerchief, tangled
parachute, now red as a candy apple,
the looming fists and faces full
of Eskimo Pies and Creamsicles.

Nostalgia, from *nostos*, returning
home, and *algos*, the pain,
as if the Greeks knew even then about
Flexi-Flyer sleds my mother wouldn't
let me have, though I watched my friend,
knees and knuckles scraping the street,
fly so low and flat he almost did
slip under the car crossing at
the bottom of our hill. Or about
that summer night my cousin
Matthew in the emergency room
surely must have known no vine
could hold that tiniest of Tarzans,
as if he saw the pickup coming

into his lane from forty years away,
how twisted and broken it would leave
us all. Or about my sister trying to run
in place on our hassock, clown
on a barrel, as though some part of her saw
how badly and yellow she would die, dwindle
like her voice the day she went
through my dream with a nickel,
and they left me to wander alone, until,
no longer bluffing, blood flooding
my brain, I stepped off blindly into space,
blindfold already fallen
from my face.

Them

How many of those '50s movies were about people
who weren't people, whose bodies had been snatched.
But the small-town someplace was always
Hollywood, the sepia night filtered day,
the spaceships plywood, the instruments just
more televisions and Christmas lights,
the monsters rubber
or daubs of paint on celluloid.
We must have been afraid
of who we were in our split-levels,
Father remote behind his newspaper,
driving the finned car to rendezvous in caves
with more of his kind, networked by telepathy,
Mother in high heels, carrying the alien seed,
looking for dust, like the heroine who
screamed so well, her rayoned breasts
ack-ack guns propped at the sky in vigilance.
They'd never let her leave town, roadblocks
everywhere, and called her crazy when she told
how her husband wasn't the man she married,
how the kid upstairs in his room
was planning to take over,
be one of them, empty
and cold as they come.

Resurrections

I never liked Easter, pale, pastel
Christmas, all that crap
candy, wax chocolate bunnies,
faux marshmallow thick
as caulk, Mike Sudan winning
the yellow baby duck by finding
stained eggs we'd have to eat
with my mother's ham—thigh
of Jacob touched by a wrestling
angel white as salt—after hours
on a hard pew. There's a picture
of me in the yard, brown
jacket, ecru pants, two-toned
shoes and bow tie, little used
car salesman. My dead sister
is tutued, hatted, net-faced,
white-gloved and socked,
just like the picture of my wife,
and a million others, all of us
pressed like dead leaves in albums
where we lie crepe-cornered and fading
between black pages, waiting to rise
and stand again in front of pink
azaleas and dogwood, young,
spruced up and slicked back,
squinting into a spring sun.

The Dead Go on Before Us

Ainie, Unkie, Ninie, Mamie: the nicknames
of my family made a hula song, those fat, diabetic,
cigar-sucking, veiny, swollen-ankled sock-givers
I saw only at Christmas. I might have been looking
at my own future, but what did I know of genes
then? My preacher father said God arranged
such things, though Jesus never had a coronary
at fifty-six, pitched headfirst into a pile
of shavings, or choked face down among fried
chicken boxes on the bathroom floor, frog-bloated
as Elvis. And his own preacher father,
my teetotal grandfather, died of cirrhosis,
and his saintly wife went mad.

I never saw Mamaw when she wasn't
shrunken in some smelly bed, first in the house
in my aunt's backyard, then a nursing home
out in the winter-bare Georgia fields.
It seemed her shriveled Cherokee smile
would speak to me, but I hid behind
my mother, who would die in a nursing home,
too. And then one by one they all died,
like her at the end, and only I
am left, beset on all sides, my own
body turned against me. Oh, great
grandmother in sheets yellow as an old
wedding dress, little girl in wrinkled
clothes and gray hat, tell me the secret
behind your smile. I'm ready to listen.

Author of the Year

Hungry for old places, names,
I ask where they're from
as I sign their books: Dalton,
Savannah, Vidalia, Sylvester,
the soft voices answer.

Were any of their parents in school
with me? If I could see even one
of my high school class, I'd know
how old I was. Instead, I have
to borrow their children to guess.

Yes, Sir, I come from Smyrna, too.

(Maybe even *her* child is here somewhere,
this honeysuckle reminding me
of hot nights on country roads.)

They think *I'm* special,
though they grow from this red clay
like sweet onions. Black faces now,
grandchildren of parents
my parents fled from into the suburbs.
And some have come from fields
where cannonball and grapeshot
are buried, like the overgrown
stones of farms that Sherman burned.
They, too, know the Bible, how it frowns
in them, how some escape, like the prodigal son.

They take me to cornbread and barbecue,
but no more moonshine, though the county's
still dry. Then past marsh and Spanish moss,
pickets of Spanish bayonet, palmetto, pine,
to the new airport to leave and go back
to late snow and dreams of soft voices,
dark faces, kudzu drive-in, honeysuckle still,
the future I didn't have, and now never will.

II

Running the Body

Cupidity

We all called him butt breath,
something inside him spoiled,
why he walked home—shambling,
pigeon-toed—from the bus stop alone.
Why, though I shot him through the cheek
with an arrow, he didn't tell
my mother, so grateful
I'd play with him.
And then he found
her, black and white,
hidden in his father's darkroom:
young, beautiful, hair
so black and thick we couldn't
see through it there
between her open legs.
We fought over her, folded her
so small to fit her hiding places
that the paper creased white, as if
she were in jail.
The final fight ripped her,
and he got the bottom. I
still have her small breasts
and face, happy to show us
all she had, her smile an arrow
in both of us forever.

Needles

She shows me how to pinch
the skin and slide it in, says
they used to siphon it
from the pancreases of pigs
to stop this withering, this
thirst of a camel on concrete.
My wife can't watch, and I, too,
think I'll faint, like those summers
Mother took me to the clinic,
tiled, art deco, free, almost overgrown
with kudzu, honeysuckle, heat,
white shapes foggy behind the rippled
walls of glass, smell of alcohol
that cooled and prickled, the fear
worse than the rusty nail in my barefoot heel
I wouldn't tell about until I woke
screaming from a dream, my jaw
locked shut. I didn't die
that time, but she warned me it was
needles kept the bad at bay, like pikes
against the pitted face of pox,
the iron lung, the slavering dog—
though too much syrup and candy
could send me back to the clinic
every day for the rest of my life.

My friends don't want to hear;
they shiver and turn away.

A hundred years ago, the doctor says,
handing it to me, *you'd be*
dead by now. I take it, silver
sliver, splinter, hair sliding
painlessly into its pore. Lightheaded,
I push the pig stuff in, smooth
and cloudy as semen.

Still Life with Chili and Onions

The way we slink here,
we might as well be wearing raincoats
with the pockets cut out.
The place is full of men, paunchy,
middle-aged—women are feeding
their hungers somewhere else.

We probably act out our youth,
Friday nights at Joe Cotton's or the Varsity
with onion rings and Byerly's orange,
the buns grilled, the chili ground fine
and peppery, tin platters propped
on the half-opened windows
of old cars that would soon be
at the drive-in movie, gravel lots
of lust and dusty honeysuckle and kudzu.
Now each sits alone in the booth
to pay for the firm
boiled dog we remember,
the mishmash of meat,
onions and their hot tears.

When we leave, guilty,
love handles grown

more useless, we go back
to our wives who ask
about our day, and we tell them
the usual, the salad,
our slippery hearts sidling
from their arms, telling lies
with our tainted breath.

Lust at Christmas

There they were, under a pile
of *Good Housekeeping*. I'd never
seen a nipple before, much less the other.
She sat cross-legged, nothing
but a fisherman's net for cover.
Back in the living room
of my uncle's house,
the adults thought my cousin and I
were playing pool, and we had been
till the ball bounced under
the bookcase. While they were
enacting our traditions—the Coke
in its curvy bottle, pimento cheese
sandwich I never ate, coconut cake
I did—we ogled like shepherds
before an angel. The woman
on the radio driving home
sang that the weather was frightful,
and the fire delightful, and later,
in bed, I prayed to the manger
that merged, then filled, with her form,
and the lights of the tree were the red
bulbs of a brothel.
I knew that Santa might
find me being bad, defiling
the birthday of baby Jesus,
but I couldn't stop, another
Herod slaughtering the innocents,
or wise man coming
to kneel before the Madonna,
bringing myrrh.

My Pills

Once a week I put my pills
in their little canoe, doling out
a seat for each day.
There's hardly room
anymore—they all
crowd in as if to sail
someplace else.

All my endocrine glands have quit.
What's the point? I can almost
hear them murmur, bubbling like divers.
Young women I stare at
don't know about my pills,
see my troubled gray hair
and think it comes this way.
Only my doctor and insurance
know about my pills, and they pull
on either end of scrip like a handsaw
pruning the trunk of my health and wealth.

If there were an accident—
the yellow oxygen masks, the long
rubbery slide into the sea—
and I washed up without them
even on some isle of brown women,
I'd be dead in a week, their nipples
undissolved on my tongue
in a brief, unhealthy heaven,
while my life raft bobbed
over the horizon
with only room for seven.

The End of Loving

Will we know it for the last time,
one of us simply taken?

Or shrug and turn away
to the business of other loosenings?

Or shake hands, the bow
of sumo after our thousands

of bouts, surging against
ourselves?

There should be a ceremony, not
a funeral, exactly, like Vikings

loading what was left of life
and shoving the burning ship

to sea, but a ritual
of tea, both kneeling

by the bed, taking
a final sip from the single

cup, then shattering the white
porcelain eggshell, so strong

only we can break it.

Greek to Me

How did those ancient tragic figures
figure out which god exactly
they'd offended?
Had they pissed, perhaps,
in Poseidon, farted in the face
of Aeolus, or so easily sinned
up against Eros? So
I flip through the card file
of prickly gods to see which
has posted me on some post
office wall of most wanting;
or, backslidden Shinto, review
the long gray line of ancestors
to find who in their photo frowns
fiercest, eyebrows cocked
like a sumo or ears back
like an angry horse. (Yes,
Mother, I *have* made fun
of you in your silken coffin.)
Or maybe just a good old Southern
Jesus, goosing me toward the noose
with my thirty dimes of dishonor
and discontent. If I knew,
I'd sacrifice, like Abraham,
my only son, if I had one,
or a virgin to a volcano,
if I knew one. No wonder

Oedipus, so het up with hubris
he didn't even recognize
ma and pa, punched out
his own lights and wobbled skittish
through the wasteland, afraid
to offend, sputtering to any possibly
supernatural stranger
he bumped into on the salted plain,
pardon.

Aesop at Sixty

Sheepish, pleading a pulled
muscle, I limp like Hephaestus
past flocks of women in white
to whisper a question. My age,
Hippocrates wipes a whisker, smiles
and gives me samples on the sly.
I stutter, *It's not that I can't . . . it's just
a question of stamina* (the sleepy
hare, the plodding tortoise). He nods.
And then, there's the mind and its mouse-
gnaw of doubt, mere cunning no
longer enough to tempt the cock
from the tree.

The insurance will pay for nine
pills a month, he says. Out of what
hat did they pull *that* number? we wonder,
and I leave with nine chances in my pocket
to be sixteen again and sense already
the snapping of that last strand
imprisoning the lion pride that once
defied my parents, time, and tide,
that feeling six inches from the tape
and the prize of Aphrodite, three-balled
with a stiff wind and Atalanta
at my back, and the certainty
that not even Zeus himself
can stop me now.

Tests

They found out what had already
happened, or hadn't, math
you either studied or didn't, declensions

of tongues you didn't know.
They're what you're still late for
in dreams, all-nighters

you pulled like a train
of your own ignorance, the wheels
slipping on the tracks.

Now they find out
what has already happened
inside you, what seeds have sprouted

crookedly, or been blown loose, swept
down dark tributaries glowing red
as tracer bullets, the blood

soured like milk in sun, cells
curdled. And then the Christmas bulb
nerves blinking like a multiple

choice, and the proctor looming
above, telling you how much time
you've got left.

Sugar

Don't you love it when you start a new
disease—the pamphlets, the prescriptions, the
attention? And the past turning
ironic, cloudy, as if you'd added
a chemical—my house painter saying he
has sugar, reminding me of my mother
demanding the sweet drool from every baby.
Until the penny dropped, and I saw
the brown monkey face of my uncle
chugging Cokes all day,
remembered how a spoonful
makes the medicine go down,
not telling my mother I'd stepped on a nail,
afraid of a needle, a spike the junkies say,
until I woke crying when I couldn't open my jaw
in a dream of eating.
Pancakes.
The syrup springing through the trees.
The sap sinking.
The reason they call it fall.

Breedlove

Where were you, my Breedlove,
my elegant guitar, when I was choked
and cramped with puberty, stiff, clumsy
fingers bleeding from hours of fondling
my Sears and Roebuck "Les Paul"?
I learned the chords before I could even tune
the thing and twanged "John Henry" and "Blowin'
in the Wind" in Japanese. Nor did
I fare better with the delicate
instrument Arleen McKee.
What I needed was a grown woman
to show me the pearl inlays, struts
and grooves, the smoothly turning keys
and lightly fingered frets of harmony.

So I apologize to Arleen, whose fault
it wasn't, though her shape, too,
symbolized my mistuned youth: big
and blonde with fertility goddess
hips and a chest well-rounded
as Monroe's or Mansfield's,
and a soundhole I could never
free the music from.

Running the Body

Until I had to balance the blood,
weigh and inject what would burn
every crumb I put into it, I never
appreciated the body. How
would it be to run
it all? Every second, squirt
of tear or saliva here, goose
of bile there while pumping
the bellows lungs, palpating
organs, remembering juices
to sluice the stomach, and always
the bowels to be squeezed along,
kidneys wrung like a sponge.
The mind's a flashing
switchboard always swamped
with what has just been sighted,
smelled, heard, sounds on the track
that projects on the old sheet
hanging back there in the dark.
And you, only two-handed when all
the lines start shrilling with fear
as the loved one draws near—
so many skills to learn! To sift
the sea-grass cilia of the nose,
to comb the coral
of the tongue, fill
the hollows with blood,
and, behind it all, an art:
the incessant and inconstant
timing of the heart.

III

Ascending Order

Mississippi Moon

Driving home from her father's house
back when we lived down here,
we'd turn the car lights off
and let the full moon silver
the road home. Sometimes we'd even
park and neck.

Back for a visit ten years along,
the skies busy approaching the millennium,
we go out into the evening to see
the eclipse like a plum with a cap
of sugar, Hale-Bopp chasing
its tail in the solar wind of the southwest,
Orion stalking the skies,
and Mars looking embarrassed
at the jewelry of Venus.

Portents all, prodigies, chimneys tumbling,
and horses eating each other in their stalls,
or at least beavers slapping the water in the dark
and rippling, like a TV time warp, the stars
and ember eyes of frogs and gators floating on the lake.
Cottonmouths sleep on logs, their mouths
full of moonlight, tired as the snake that swallowed
its tail and made the world, and turtles—like the one
the Natives say the world rests on the back of—
poke their heads from the lake like toes.

No wonder people dream of abduction
by aliens on lonely back roads, city lights
so far way, these stars we thought we knew
moving farther from us and from each other.
So when a comet comes calling every
4,000 years or so, we go out and hold hands,
our faces upturned and white as two more moons,
Mars puts blusher over his cracks,
the moon veils her pitted face
and hides her belly with a dark muumuu,
Venus scintillates desperately,
and Orion loosens his belt and holds on,
none of us getting any younger.

The Poet, Calling the Kettle Black

I name to myself my students
as if we were all Indians—
to my left, the beautiful
Two Kids in Play School,
in front, the shaggy
Car Won't Start,
to my right, the timid
Cries over Commas.
Perhaps because a student says
I was her Hopi father
in another life,
this comes naturally to me, and I
expect to overhear in the men's room
complaints about old Dry as Dust,
or Where Was I, or
Sleep Bringer.

My sister was Jelly Side Down,
my brother, No Forwarding Address,
and where would I be without my love,
It's My Fault?

I can almost remember being rocked
to sleep each night after I had climbed
into my cliff house,
my mother, Cry More and You'll Pee Less,
fighting with her husband, Will
of God, then crooning lullabies
to little If He'd Set Out to Fail,
He Could Not Have Done Worse.

The Punishment of Days

There are days beyond
salvation, the day my wife
almost died, the Sunday
my father did, strewing
even the floors of sleep
with broken glass.

It's not enough to say
thank God *that* day
is done. No,
there should be a place
to send them, an
island, guards sweating
and unbuttoned, sharks
prowling the jagged coast.

But because the crater of my bad day
might be ground zero for some blessed birth,
the sidewalk outline of my heart
the stepping stone of someone's
coming home, my cross
the busy intersection of
the accidents of love,

I would not damn the days
of everyone, though mine
would burn like the passengers
of a ship that's gone aground,
even the water on fire.

Priscilla

for Patty

My student, who has been "regressed"
many times, through all her other lives,
says she knew me on a ship, and we
were married, though not to each other.
The ship went down, and I, a woman,
got put on a lifeboat with my children.
She, a man, drowned saving the children
of others. She says my child is now
her nephew, shows me his photo
to see if I recognize him (her?). I don't,
but tell her this means nothing since
I'm the least transmigratory
of any soul I know—although
it's only noon, I'm thinking of
a heaven of martinis after a day
of work.

Being a woman living long ago,
I never got the insurance money
I was owed. *Maybe that's why*
you've got poetry now, she says.
I don't disbelieve any of this.
In fact, tonight I'll try to have a drink
with her, try hard to remember her face
in a sea-salt tarnished mirror,
or the faces of children. Perhaps

I'll begin to dream of her, a "breakthrough"—
she'll wander through my house at night,
wondering over TVs and tapping keyboards,
while I marvel at the pewter ruffles
of the silk dress where a small, wet head
wept between my breasts.

The Last Annual Dead Celebrity Charity Golf Tournament

Napoleon kept trying to drive
the green, coming up short,
then trudging back to try again.
Hitler wouldn't come out
of the first bunker,
and Amelia Earhart, well,
she hasn't been seen since Jack
followed his slice into
the woods behind her. The only limbs
the search party found
were in the bushes and still attached
to Casanova, making a hole in one
with Catherine the Great, who also
got Bogie.
The Marquis de Sade and Lucretia Borgia,
who cheats like hell, made a threesome
with Delilah, and Samson really could
drive the green.
Milton, Helen Keller, and Homer, who had
the biggest handicaps, didn't get back
till after dark.
Jane Austen and Virginia Woolf
never even left their cart,
just sat talking in floppy hats,
and Ghandi and Buddha just sat.

Putting Lewis with Clark
was a bad idea, claiming they'd won
because they hacked a path from the 5th to the 18th.
Cleopatra, Caesar, and Shakespeare got drunk,
scuffed the greens, bent clubs,
hit other people's balls.
Bobby Jones and Jesus tied, of course,
and Jesus won in sudden death.
Except for Lincoln,
nobody raked the traps,
filled their divots,
or replaced the flags.
And nothing was raised for the living.

Prostrate

When the barber sees my hair, his eyes
widen, his ancient clippers pause in the air,
humming like flies' wings. I bring her father,
hobbling with a cane, among these old
Mississippi farmers wearing overalls
and white socks, to trim his gray fringe.
It's like a general store, and they talk
of guns and deer, crops and weather,
their joints and scars and the sawing
through breastbones, while I look at *People*
and the walls of rifles and plows,
the hung, gray, papery wasps' nests
swollen around their limbs,
and lots of antlers, the splay
of rattlers' skins. Two artillery shells
stand waist-high in the corner, and I think
of the rubber catheter squirming loose
and slippery as a tentacle, the blood
on his underwear and sheets, my dreams
of erections, liver-spotted.
The barber says,
like a TV evangelist or Bible prophet,
I don't care what you do, if you're
man of woman born you will not get out
of this life without prostrate.
After a mere twelve minutes and the four
dollars it's always been, I lead her father
away like the blind Samson, the others
watching, the only sound now the buzzing
that makes their short hair shorter.

Ascending Order

Though it never does much good,
souls clear as bottles
come to be recycled,
wanting to be filled again
with personality.
Hemophiliacs trundle
their metal saplings
of transfusion behind them,
emotions dark and dripping,
where men who've murdered their wives
look at paint samples,
while saints, imprisoned
in their modesty, squirm
in the corners of the waiting room,
and Penelopes, humming,
weave and unweave their travesties.

Dreaming *Gone with the Wind*

Again tonight I whip the flagging,
frothing mule down red clay roads,
through the ruts of battlefields, over
limbs of men and under buzzards, back
to Georgia. At the half-burnt house, white
columns sooted black, my father, dazed,
meets me at the door, my name
forgotten, my mother dead
in the dark parlor, propped between candles.
I know I'll never go hungry again
for dreams or memories.

I took all my friends, rode into
downtown Atlanta on the bus, black
people in the rear, to the Loew's
Grand where it premiered, on Peachtree
only steps from where a taxi ran
Margaret Mitchell down. And then
to the Cyclorama, big
museum of the battle, all around us
in paint and plaster, hills of splintered
pines, skeins of smoke, blooms
of cannon fire, guns, the sundered
bodies of blue and gray.

It happened the other way
around—my father dying, my mother

mindless, wandering from room
to room, forgetting my name.
And I live up North, dream my war,
my nightly journey that never
seems to end, a Cyclorama scene—
drunken Grant and pious Lee
glaring over corpses,
the courthouse famous and empty
in between.

Hell's Garage

When you first come in, you see
Casanova's Probe, jacked up,
front tires off and clawing
like a crab, cracked seats from all
the chicks, oil pan dripping, dipstick
gone, hood open like a mouth
at the dentist, ragtop ripped
and showing through.

It's dark all the time, greeny oil
puddled in the shadows, the only light
those bare bulbs they hang from the ribs
of rafters. No car ever leaves, much less
leaves fixed, and where would they go
since they're already over the hill?—
these stretch limos of rock stars,
moonshine runners with the extra tank,
low riders of pimps, Hitler's
Volkswagen, Custer's Dakota.
While they hear up above,
flying around the roads of heaven,
Stravinsky's Firebird, Homer's
Odyssey, Shelley's Skylark,
even Shakespeare's old Tempest,
and God, not in some Millenia,
too small for his immensities,
but behind the wheels within wheels

of a Cadillac with the Northstar engine,
little dog in the back nodding *Yes, Yes,*
plastic Jesus on the dash, radio tuned to
and turned up on Nonstop Hits of the '50s,
exhaust fumes like a sweet Havana,
and a sunroof that He might shine
on all creation and burn
rubber on the wet pavements
of the Milky Way.

Flock

Once, walking these backroads of Mississippi,
headphones on high, I saw something
rare and wondrous strange—goats,
white as clouds or angels, with cocker ears,
grazing by a red-dirt pond bulldozed
in a field, and so exotic a sight
gave me heart in this land of all-
you-care-to-cram catfish, pickup
trucks, and tornadoes, the people
stringy and hookwormed even
under their dessert bar fat, the look
my mother called "country," a race
whose graven images of ATVs, water
towers, and satellite dishes take the place
of old-growth forest I've seen in photos.
Now even the second- and third-
growth has gone, felled and milled, more
catty-corners cleared for the face-off
of banks and Baptist churches, the beetled
bark of what's left stapled with signs,
Are You Ready for the Rapture?
and I wake each morning to the birdsong
of buzz saws. So today when I walked
that road again, I wanted to see
more than the dam broken,
the blood-red pond drained and mud-slick,
the goats gone, as if their ears had
flapped them up to a better state, leaving us
fallen and fat in a thin land.

The Tire of Babel

. . . and the Lord God destroyed the tires of Babylon . . .
—*a radio evangelist, of 9/11*

Who hath purposed this against Tyre, the bestower of
crowns, whose merchants are princes, whose traffickers
are the honorable of the earth?
—*Isaiah 23:8*

I think he has confused Babel
with that ziggurat of luxury, the Hanging
Gardens, or the Whore, of Babylon,
or perhaps the burning topless towers
of Ilium. But maybe he does mean
tires, the way their zigzag tread
murmurs to me even now, in the lull
between towns, late, after hours
of high-beam blacktop, following the stutter
of white lines, the voices changing
like stations—another pipsqueak
preacher, sometimes a wife, then
a mother, father, football coach—
though all their advice stays the same
and still contradicts, arguing with
each other: just more static, more
babble about Babylon, Zion, or even Tyre,
the best route to somewhere else, or
some dumb way to climb higher.

Dead Mouse Car

She drives the big one, the Enterprise,
gas guzzler, a/c, power steering
like slithering through butter,
gliding out of the garage and into Magellanic clouds.
I get the Shuttle, with a stick, some rust,
but good gas mileage.
And a dead mouse inside somewhere.
He probably thought
he'd made a find—uptown, dry,
dark, warm, and nobody else
in the building.

At first, instead of the pure air
of outside, there was fluff, fur,
and leafmeal. And then
the smell.
Now it's summer, and I drive with
the windows open, but when winter comes
I'll have to use the fan, unblock the vents
to let it fill the car. Maybe
I'll put something on the stereo
to ease his way, something about going out
in style, Lyle Lovett doing "Swing Low,
Sweet Chariot," headed for that
fuzzy nest in the dark between the stars,
and sure to get there
with so many miles to the gallon.

Climbing Mount Wilson

The Mansons had just murdered Sharon Tate,
and there we were wandering dead drunk
past midnight in those same foothills and canyons,

my Navy buddy determined to show me,
hick from Georgia, the view from up high,
when we looked down from the rickety bridge to see

sheeted figures walking
silently, single file, along the stones
of a dry creek bed.

It isn't easy to run
noiseless, backpacked,
and breathless up a rocky, moon-white road

through ax-wielding cactus and witch-fingered
sage, and so we lay a long time
panting beneath the observatory

looking up at the spilled stars until, almost
sober, we unpacked the wine and began
drinking again, looking down at the constellation

of L.A., Hubbell's big cosmic
cannon pointing from the egg above
our heads at who knows what,

and we drank until we felt the universe
explode in the Big Bang of Boone's Farm
Strawberry, and we yelled to no one there,

Let there be light, and there was,
and we woke in it, alive, unaxed,
lying on picnic tables and aching all over

as if we'd been dropped
from the sky, around us empty
bottles broken and glittering.

Waiting in the Flu Line

The first ten yards aren't bad, tall
plastic columns of colored candy
on one side of the aisle, humorous
greeting cards on the other that we reach
for and read, chuckling, shaking our heads,
shuffling through fluorescence. It's
"At Risk" day, and though I'm diabetic,
the others look suspiciously at my relative
youth or low body fat. But that
winter my wife lay in our tiny bed
and I on the floor in another room, both
too weak to even cook a can of soup,
until finally a friend brought food
and ice cream, the melting scoops little
clown faces with M&M noses
and dunce-cap cones.

Now I'm up to the serious cards,
condolences for death and disease,
and there's nowhere to look but
up ahead to more candy wall or the gum-wad
hearing aid in the ear in front, until
we reach the religious cards of crosses, lilies,
and angels. Everyone seems to know
everyone else, the couples hold
hands, and I wonder if it will feel
this way in the long line down
to the landing as we wait to board
the boat, if I will be alone

there, too, my useless arms finally
needed for a child, which I will have
to hand to the ferryman while I
stoop to drink, inoculation
against what I might carry
across, memories so beautiful
they are impossible to bear.

IV

Man Goeth to His Long Home

Natural History

There is a peculiar agony in the paradox that truth has two forms, each of them indisputable, yet each antagonistic to the other.
—Edmund Gosse, Father and Son

The museum guide brings up the past
in me, still the student who made good
eye contact, always asking another
question, while my whispers had
the teacher frowning and wondering
what she had said that was so funny.
And then another of her notes
to my father with his Bible-black strop.

His memory looms like a ghost
barring me from the room
of dinosaurs, where,
above the babble of school children
on an outing, I hear the shouting
of our arguments again, about the "frauds"
of bones fished from different graves
and glued together, how the world was created
at ten o'clock on Wednesday morning,
4004 B.C., and not an hour
earlier. I look at the giant skulls
intact atop the long ladder
of interlocking little bones, fifty
yards from tooth to tail tip,
and know that even this
wouldn't change his mind, show him

a different god, because he knew
"for a fact" that Clarence Darrow
was an atheist, a liberal, and
an intellectual, who believed,
against the word of God,
only what death had dropped to bloom
the sand of sea bottoms, or stamped
in strata of river clay, sculpted
in shale.

What does this museum resemble?
the guide asks, and we, obedient, murmur
together what is obvious: a cathedral, all
stained glass and vaulting, where Victorians
worshipped the infinite variety of God
that floated on the flood in pairs
above the mud that covered bones
of monkeys, stunted men, and murdered children
now dug up and strung on end to stand
as our stooped old fathers, extinct,
and never to be seen again.

In the National Gallery

Houses in shadow, is the sun
rising or going down, the warmth
nearing or draining from you,
and are the trees hung with last leaves
or the colored flags of a spring flood?
This brook either paints itself in
like a ceiling with fresh coats
of mountain water, icing to the mud,
or melts, unbacking a mirror of its own quick
silver to show again a bottom
of silt and stone. The sun
is moving some way, that much
must be true, but is it slicing the darkness
away in shives like the Sunday roast
or adding another onionskin of shade?

So paintings refuse to look forward
or back, no memory or prophecy,
no warning or excuse,
admitting only the moment, not
how the gauzy apple came to be,
or whether a hand will pick it
from the plate and eat, or let it
rot, the way in Vernet's *The Battle of Jamappes*
the outcome is not shown, only
the general on his ivory horse
poised on a hill against the balanced
white of a distant windmill,

and in the valley between, tulips
of bleeding soldiers, lilies
of shell smoke under bruised clouds
that either approach to quench the fires of battle,
or recede like foam on the sand
to leave behind an evening of benign
and barbarous light.

Michelangelo's Erection

The first time I ever saw
the Sistine Chapel was in
the church library in Atlanta,
Georgia. Someone had screwed
up, but we kept the secret from
the deacons and our mothers, who
were pleased we were so
interested in art.

Did Brenda Wilkie look
like this, with broad shoulders
beneath her choir robe, that plump
pear, hairless, between her thighs?
Did Michelangelo lie on his back
beneath creation, bristling days and nights
to make those breasts and buttocks, all
for the glory of God, just so we
could fight to bend over
the book for hours?

I still tend to look for the nudes
on every wall, and never leave a museum
without a hard-on like a statue, not
a smutty Southern Baptist boner, more
Greek, of nymphs and satyrs.
Recently, they restored the Sistine
ceiling, the women coming clean
from beneath the stains
that always made sense to me.

The Toilets of Cathedrals

They've had to add them on to all
the centuries, cram them in the cloister walls

or crypts, pipe hot water in, hand-drying air.
Stained glass windows are upstairs,

downstairs the hidden porcelain grail,
the mirror's haloed face, fluorescent, pale.

Up there the vaulted roof's so high
it gathers in a private sky,

but paneless windows down below
look in on only catacombs to show

an ancient skeleton made of stones
with plumbing squirming through the bones.

This is where we go to preen and purge
and lighten and renew the spirit's urge

to be the airy thing our bodies never could,
but also to remind ourselves that flesh is good,

that if there were a brothel underneath,
these appetites might spawn a new belief,

cathedral underground, below the waist,
with niches for the saints of the unchaste,

and make a single porcelain image from
those icons of the double kingdom come—

Our Lady of Electricity, kneeling in prayer
to the rubber Baby Jesus with Real Hair.

Tyson's Pygmy

Those were the days when everything
was still to be named, when that Mantell
woman picked, from a pile of road stones,
bones that she called
dinosaur. So when Tyson saw
the little skeleton, intact
but for the wired-
together skull, the long
funny bone and radius
hanging down below the knees,
who can blame him for remembering
rumors of pygmies, and putting two
and two together
to get three? It was, in fact, a baby
chimp, that, playing in the rigging
on the voyage from Africa, fell
on a cannon and died of a shattered jaw.

When Tyson called it what he wished, instead
of what he saw, he became a scientist
no more, just the maker of a manikin,
as if he could hope a human
into being, as if, in the beginning,
the idea had us, and we grew
from its ground like grains the storm
blew to this local place.
Light years later, gale forces
push us farther still, and still
we try to wrest our destiny away,
wishing forearms, foreheads, hearts bigger,
the better to become what we say.

The Leg of Mutton Nude

In Cookham village, where he painted
Christ preaching from the bank

of the Thames to the crowd sprawled
around in punts, drinking beer

and lemonade, arrayed
in Panama hats and Edwardian gowns,

Stanley Spencer planned a building
like a body lying on the ground, "The Church

of Me." Its naves, niches, alcoves,
and apses would hold his life like

a body its dreams and memories, one
chapel for the wife of his youth, her portraits

hung above votive candles, the colors
bleeding and glowing, casting

stained glass on the walls. Another
room would be devoted to

the woman he left her for, the bogus
artist who married him for money

to live with her lesbian lover
whose paintings she cribbed and called

her own. She never gave him her
body except in oils, the two of them

always wrinkled and bare, she, in one,
reclining in the middle ground, sallow

skin and sagging breasts, pubic bush
jutting from a juncture of bony thigh,

hands behind her head, smiling smugly.
A leg of mutton in the foreground rhymes

her body, while he sits behind,
nude and hangdog, hungry, long

cock limp as he contemplates
the meat. In another, she's curled

in the background, swollen stomach
overlaid by the back of his shoulders

and head, which is turned toward
but not looking at her. Backward

portrait, double mirror view, he's
roosterish with beaky nose and craning

neck, squinting above his spectacles,
elfin ears pricked as if he hears

the high-heeled step of one
who'd have no room in his church,

apostate, skulking Judas, shy
sculptor taking and molding, bending

the pliable, welding what doesn't
go together, like Spencer himself,

always warping what was there, seeing
what he believed instead, as when

he painted Christ carrying his cross
down the High Street of Cookham,

the villagers, sorrowful, leaning
and looking down from their upstairs

windows, chintz curtains blowing out
on either side of them like wings.

First Impression

I don't look like anyone, but
a woman I met the other day
called me Liam Neeson, though
she said it Lie Am, my star's face
slightly askew like the slew of a stick
thrust through the torque of water,
the Roman nose of a boxer pushed aside
by a Picasso punch. We all
have a double somewhere, they say,
maybe the other side of someone else's
wonderful life, a poor man's Jimmy Stewart
who takes the rap for embezzlement and falls
just short of what is wanted, another
beautiful face, but squinted through
the smudge of a thumbprint glass,
faded like a photo taken from
the amniotic developer too soon.
Even Adam with his matinee curls,
reclining on the rolled and pleated couch
of clay on the Sistine ceiling, is not
being touched by the finger of God, but,
by a trick of perspective, pointed
past, to what He *really* meant: not you,
Adam, with your orangutan arms and tree-thick
trunk, but him, him back there, the willowy
pretty boy right behind you.

Ennui

Trying to impress the woman I
would marry, I sighed and said
(never having heard the word,
only read it in books), *I'm filled
with in-you-I.* She, who'd been
to France, said, *Pardon?*

Maybe that was Freudian then,
but now I know it as the universal
principle, from the planets in their ruts,
to the stars shunning each other
like guests at a cocktail party, sidling
away as if they could find a better
universe to talk to, without the wanking
apes at the zoo, the yawning
lions on the Serengeti.

It's the companion that huffily
withdraws whenever the glamour
girls of death and danger approach
with their snaky hair, and then returns
when they've left, comes sulking
back, lipstick smeared, cigarette bent
in its holder, same old peignoir
of ostrich plumes.

In Sickert's *Ennui*, a couple
occupies a room without doors
or windows—she stands and stares

at stuffed birds in a bell jar,
he sits at a bare table,
puffing a cigar, their backs
to each other. What we see
are the browns and grays, but not
what they see, perhaps another life,
like a planet where the lions are tame
and the apes speak French, and comets
approach with their cocktails and ostrich
plumes of flame.

Man Goeth to His Long Home

... because man goeth to his long home,
and the mourners go about the streets.
—Ecclesiastes 12:5

In the painting, Stanley Spencer has shown us
only the white bulk of a man, facing away,
triangular as the fir he stands before, so
evergreen we might almost remember it
festooned with lights, but layered here
with shade and overlaid with the larger shadow
of this Biblical figure, white-robed, long-haired,
haunting Cookham village; his bent right
knee tents his robe where he places one
sandaled foot on a hillock, as if he would
climb it and go beyond, to where he looks,
his head with its wounded wing of hair
turned toward a distant sunlit orchard.
Behind him, in the foreground in front of us,
sprouts the stone mushroom of a bollard
whose thin arms of chain mark the corner
of what must be a grave; it throws a squat
shadow ahead. Another shadow of something
off-screen in the lower left advances
on the man but has not yet arrived.

But the tree and the chain fence have been added,
my program says, and thus the little chess rook,
too, that guards a corner of the grave we can't quite see,
and this view looks not from the vantage of a churchyard,

but "south from the corner of Carter's shed by
Lambert's stables," the way he painted
the Annunciation in the schoolhouse with
a view of the pub, Zaccheus watching Jesus
from the monkey puzzle tree, and Christ
preaching to the Cookham Regatta.

So why this tree, without a dangling tax collector
or parabolic figs, mimicking the man? Invented
yew, shaggy mammoth of a graveyard never seen,
you must have been newly planted by art to block
the view of the worst of the village,
or to show the first tree and man,
made ripe with shadow and ever green.

White Buildings by Water
with Steps Going Down

This scene of my dreams
in so many paintings, even the ruins
ruins of a place I remember
whole, the little bay always opening on
the setting sun. Turner
felt it, too, and asked that his
Dido Building Carthage always
share a room with Lorain's *The Seaport*.
How similar they are, huge, their suns
in your eyes but scarfed in golden
cloud, on either side the white
stone buildings among emerald trees,
steps going down into the clear
sea of lapis lazuli, where
children sometimes swim,
while men in robes on the quay
hold disquisition with the sun,
pointing to the place where it will set,
as if the artists all were painting
a place they'd seen, or maybe just
remembered, a port
safe from the many-headed
hydra of history, where once a ship
sailed from some place as lovely
as death, and brought them back
to life once more.

V

Fell Walking in Long Light

Stick Figures in a Landscape

Carreg Cennan Castle, Wales

We climb to hilltop history,
ants to the far-off viewer, crawling
this medieval ruin sprawling
in defeat. Once men in victory

came with steel to smash the granite crown,
unweave rebellion's stony warp and weft,
but it outlasted them, and this is all that's left
of the building up and then the tearing down.

Three wimpled women in archaic dresses
sit and sew before a jousting tent
with flying flags; a falcon seems content
to wait, its talons tied, for now, with jesses.

Then she shows a battle-ax and arrowheads
that hook and jag to tear the screams
from men, as the walls we walk to streamed
with boiling oil, and crossbows took dead

aim through crosses cut in stone—
flesh hiding in and charging toward
the hard facts of the world, their patriotic rhetoric ignored
in the argument of iron with flesh and bone.

As we return the way we came,
we meet some youngsters rising toward our height—

they've come to see this lofty sight,
this citadel of earthly fame,

have followed through the farmyard at the foot,
where pecking peacocks strut and preen
as though the world has never seen
such motleyed immortality. They know God put

them here to raise their colors over rust,
to break with flesh the stones of time,
their greens and blues transforming grime
to gold, and all that is untrue, to dust.

Halloween in Wales

Not a pumpkin to be seen
here twenty years ago, but now they leer
from everywhere at us, who knew
corn sheaves and covered bridges,
tree-lined country roads like tunnels
through flame, bobbing
Winesaps, and Little
Orphant Annie sweeping up
the supper crumbs.

But let them have their goblins
back, who invented banshees, witches
hovering on the heaths, the stags'
heads of ancient Druids, wicker men
and Green Man golems, fairies, the flibbertigibbet
of bats. God knows they have
the props: fog and mist and
moaning wind, castles chock-a-block
with ghosts and all the ghastly forms
of flesh, of what we feel and fear
inside, down the road the cottage where
a hangman hanged himself,
and the hill where a preacher burned
a baby, offspring of his sin.

But we miss the children begging candy,
the comic danger of stumbling spooks
believing completely what they've become,
my sister in a tutu, a cape that finally
let me fly, the certain knowledge

that sweetness dwelt in every house.
Here, we wait for Guy Fawkes, stuffed
and mortal man, the Old Guy children ask
a penny for. To celebrate his not
killing when he meant to kill,
they gather all the scraps,
carry them to the highest spots,
then pile them up and put on top
a man of straw and light the fires
and dance and whoop, and every hill
burns like a baby.

Pennyhitch Hill

Here lies Mary wife
of James Kavanaugh
of Penmaen who
was murdered by

on 3rd of Oct. 1829
aged 75 years.

For a penny, the old guy would hitch
his heavy horse to yours and haul,
up through the steep and twisting
leaflit tunnel, under gnarls of oak
and beech, whatever barley, beer, or contraband
could be auctioned at the little village
green above the bay, beneath
the cross that's gone now,
the flint socket of the crier's stone
empty as an eye.

In the churchyard, just up the lane
from Hangman's Cross—where they hanged
the ones whose guilt was proved, confessed,
or guessed—stands the murderer's stone.
And, since this is Wales, it's carved with a blank
to draw the murdering conscience back
up the hill at night, past groaning trees,
no one awake or alive to help
hoist the heavy sin.

Mary's name has almost gone,
ravens, without the gorge

of rotting flesh, beg tourist crusts,
and a sheepdog with no sheep corrals
the pasture every hour, tries
to herd the horses grazing
at peace and ignorant.
At night, in the bat-squeak silence
beneath the belfry clock, you can
almost hear the cries of the hanged,
damned, and doomed, and the moans
of one who forever kneels
and tries with spectral hands
to scratch his name in stone.

Before the Fire

The man goes first, kneels
before the fire in front of her, feels
her belly rising faster
and faster against his brow. Then
she kneels in chiaroscuro, half
holds the blaze as an apple blush,
the bottle-top moan of wind across
the chimney's mouth letting
a genie out.

Theirs is the prettiest village
in England, the river so clear
that only the wavering watercress, flotsam
of fallen leaves, and ducks give it away,
then scrims of cottages, golden-stoned,
late autumnal orchards gauzed
with mist, turquoise, peach-clouded
skyline silhouettes of trees.

Though they are probably through
for good, they're trying one more
time—vinegar moon—walking
hand-in-hand the boot-squelch
footpaths past the chilly folds
fleecy with sheep, and sitting
by the fire she tends until
the logs burn down to embers
that feed each other a final flame
before they fall to the ashes
something might rise from.

The Celtic Men's Club

We flinch when anywhere near
authority, in the sun smear

unguents on our ashen skins,
struggle with liquor, sex, and other sins

of Christian guilt we lug like golf bags, shirking
while we should be on campus working,

teaching the great, male, Anglo-Saxon dead,
while all the time rehearsing in our heads

guitar chords, latest bodhran hits,
or squeezing squeals from bagpipe tits,

and dreaming beer foam, beads
of drizzle on our silly hats and tweeds

brought home from British brakes and braes,
reminders of Druidic glory days

before we fled the English, or the stranger
long-haired, dark-skinned danger,

retreated until out of reach
into the fens and fastnesses of tribal speech.

We've lost three countries, maybe four;
what matters if we lose one more?

Ponies on the Skyline

*The wild ponies of Wales are said to warn farmers of
impending storms by the manner in which they graze the
moors.*
—Welsh folklore

Sometimes the saws of country lore
(*once the devil has ridden by and spit*
on the blackberries in October,
don't pick or eat them anymore)

hold true, like how to read the sky,
as cows and sheep lie down
and shelter under pastured trees
to keep their udders clean and dry

when storms begin to lurk
behind the hills, and spiders in the morning know
that rain would squander, heave, unweave
their nightlong web of work.

I like the tale of the ponies best,
and watch for them on watch
for the first of the clouds that we can't see
amassing in the west,

who faithfully stand through gathering gloom,
outline themselves against the purple clouds,
let lightning flash them steady on,
knee deep in heather, gorse, and broom.

They could be down in hidden combes,
out of the wind, the grasses green and thick,
instead of etched along the bare horizon,
like silhouettes of stone-age tombs.

It's said they never sleep, but keep awake,
don't whinny their complaint, but stay
stolid on the humps of hills, and meet
the sky halfway, for human sake.

O'Carolan's Farewell to Music

for Delyth

These sounds bring outside in
to this old church, keening of wind

on moor and mountain, raindrops
darkly rippling tarns and loughs;

their catgut lifts us, as stones were hauled,
stacked, and leveled to lift these walls

until they met the timbers patterned, spread
like earth-grown heavens overhead.

Old with whiskey and harp-songs through
all of middle earth, O'Carolan one day knew

he must die, though above the rood screen as she plays,
Jesus perches painted by the dying light of day

through stained-glass figures whose voices blend
and sing along in light that bends

but never breaks,
their crystal bodies colors of a wake

that never ends.

Fell Walking in Long Light

For forty years we've wandered hills,
pillars of cloud across our path,
a yolk of sun breaking through
to guide us, tea by the cold
tarns as the evening peaks
declined into violet below
the rising moon, have gone back
down as daylight sank behind
the silhouette of scenery.

Now, footsore, we know
we don't have many mountains
in us anymore, that now
it's evening in the valleys,
remembering how the sun
warmed us on the hills.
But late in the day the light
comes slanting across the fields,
pouring honey over green,
and every sheep is a burning bush.

Toad's Wild Ride

And as you are American, I would like you to pay
special attention to the turn signal indicator.
—English rental car agent, 1978

A motorcar, a motorcar, wheezed Toad,
sitting unhorsed and dazed in the dust,
then bought his own snorting, sneezing
thing. First time in England, fifty
thousand miles ago, they handed us keys,
showed us everything backwards,
then walked away. *What in God's name!*
I yelled at my first roundabout, a whirlpool
of tiny traffic instead of a stoplight (we trust
inertia, they trust momentum). But,
by the end of the trip, I felt like donning
duster, goggles, scarf, could brush and burnish
oncoming cars with my whoosh of onionskin air.
Cheerio, we'd cry as we careened around a turn, as if
headed for Badger's house in the Wild Wood.

For twenty years, we've taken one-track
roads, dotted on the map like pinholes
in pie crust, backing up for tractors,
even for horses and dog walkers, though
it's not for tourist cars these banked and tunneled
turns were made, but sports cars curved
and swooping like Spitfires, exhaust
thudding off stone walls and hedgerows, swallows
and swifts weaving the wind just ahead of the bonnet,
dolphin surfing the prow-push of bug-flushing, flower-scented air.

Though we're no sports, we've goosed our share
of farmyard geese, scattered village swans and swains
neighed the horses and boomed through woods
past country things, the sidelong flash
of fox, skirr of pheasant. And when we get
frog fat and old, we'll take tour buses,
lumber the lanes, frighten cars of
young couples to vanish in reverse,
and look down on all we used to make
fly up like the driven dust we are.

About the Author

William Greenway, a native of Georgia with a B.A. from Georgia State University and a Ph.D. from Tulane University, is professor of English at Youngstown State University. He has published four full-length collections of poetry, most recently *Simmer Dim* in the Akron Series in Poetry. For the same series, Greenway co-edited with Elton Glaser *I Have My Own Song For It: Modern Poems of Ohio*. He was 1994 Georgia Author of the Year and has won the Ohioana Poetry Award, the Larry Levis Editors' Prize from *Missouri Review,* the Open Voice Poetry Award from The Writer's Voice, the State Street Press Chapbook Competition, and an Ohio Arts Council Fellowship.

About the Book

Ascending Order was designed and typeset by Amy Petersen. The cover was designed and typeset by Jodi Arment. *Ascending Order* was printed on 60-pound Glatfelter and bound by Cushing-Malloy of Ann Arbor, Michigan.